It's my BIRTHDAY!

WRITTEN BY
SHARI LAST

It's my birthday and I remember the moment I wake up!

It's my birthday and I can't wait for my party!

It's my birthday and I wonder what's inside my present!

It's my birthday and I'm going to play with Grandpa.

It's our birthday which means balloons!

It's my birthday and I'm in charge!

It's my birthday and
I'm having the best day!

It's my birthday and I get to blow out the candle!

It's my birthday and everyone is nice to me.

It's my birthday and I'm going to eat so much cake!

It's my birthday so there's confetti all over the place.

It's my birthday which means surprises.

It's my birthday and now I'm big!

There is no ONE way to celebrate your birthday.
There is no one way to do ANYTHING!

How would you describe yourself?

I am _____

I am _____

I am _____

Write down three things that make you YOU!

1.

2.

3.

First published in Great Britain in 2024
Cupcake Press,
an imprint of
TELL ME MORE Books

Text copyright ©2024 Shari Last
Design copyright ©2024 Shari Last

ISBN: 978-1-917200-12-7

Picture credits: Thanks to Adobe Stock.

All rights reserved. Without limiting the rights under the copyright reserved above, no part of this publication may be reproduced, stored in, or introduced into a retrieval system, or transmitted, in any form, or by any means (electronic, mechanical, photocopying, recording or otherwise), without the prior written permission of the copyright owner.

CUPCAKE PRESS

Visit our website:
www.tellmemorebooks.com

www.ingramcontent.com/pod-product-compliance
Lightning Source LLC
Chambersburg PA
CBHW050749110526
44591CB00002B/27